LEAVING CHARLESTON HARBOR

The Legend of ROBERT SMALLS

WRITTEN BY
DONALD N. WATSON

ILLUSTRATED BY
JAROB BRAMLETT
OF QUIET STRENGTH DESIGN

Thea Harris Publishing Inc.
P.O. Box 7576
Port St. Lucie, FL 34985
www.theaharrispublishing.com

This book is dedicated to all freedom fighters from Moses and Aaron to T. C. Watson, Sr., Ben Watson, Caroline Edwards and beyond.

Leaving Charleston Harbor

©2022 by Donald Watson

Illustrated by Jarob Bramlett of Quiet Strength Designs, LLC

All rights reserved. No portion of this book may be reproduced, stored in a retrieval system, or transmitted in any form or by any means - electronic, mechanical, photocopying, recording, scanning or other, except for brief quotation in critical reviews or articles, without the prior written permission of the publisher.

ISBN 978-0-9909170-6-9

Printed in the United States of America

Sound the horn in Charleston Harbor.
 Robert Smalls is coming through.

Born enslaved in South Carolina, Robert knew what he must do.

When the Captain left the Planter,
        Spent the night upon the shore,

Robert donned the Captain's clothing,
	Soon to be enslaved no more.

As he steered throughout the harbor,
Robert had to stay low key,

Until they reached the Union Blockade.
Robert then knew he was free!

Open up the doors of Congress!
Robert Smalls is coming in.

Businessman and Politician.
 Many races he would win.

Open up the doors of freedom!
    They've been locked for much too long!

Robert broke off chains that bound him.
He was good and brave and strong.

Robert Smalls was such a genius,
　　　　　　Carried out his brilliant plan.

He escaped the South's oppression,
 Fought for freedom in our land.

He was part of Reconstruction;
He did much for one and all.

Learn

&

Test Your

Knowledge

TWELVE INTERESTING FACTS ABOUT ROBERT SMALLS*

1. **Robert Smalls was born on April 5, 1839 in Beaufort, South Carolina, in a cabin behind his master's house.**

2. **In 1856, at the age of seventeen, Robert married Hannah Jones, an enslaved maid.**

3. **Robert saved up one-hundred dollars to pay for freedom for his wife and their children, but he was still seven-hundred dollars short of the cost.**

4. **When Robert told his wife about his plans to escape, Hannah stated, "It is a risk, dear, but you and I and our little ones must be free. I will go, for where you die, I will die."**

5. **Correctly using the hand signals he had learned, Robert Smalls guided the ship, the Planter, past five Confederate harbor ports, without the Planter being fired upon.**

6. As the Planter approached the USS Onward, near the end of its escape journey, Robert Smalls took off his straw hat and said to the Captain of the Onward, *"Good Morning, Sir! I have brought you some of the Old United States guns, Sir!"*

7. Through a bill passed by the U. S. Congress, Robert Smalls received $1500.00 (equivalent to about $40,715.00 in 2021) of the prize money for the Planter.

8. After the daring escape, Robert Smalls served in the United States Navy and fought in several battles during the Civil War.

9. After the war, Robert purchased his former master's house at 511 Prince Street.

10. Robert Smalls was elected to both the South Carolina House of Representatives and the U.S. Congress. In the South Carolina legislature, he made the statement, *"My race needs no special defense, for the past history of them in this country proves them to be the equal of any people anywhere. All they need is an equal chance in the battle of life."* These words are inscribed on a monument to Robert Smalls in the church plot where he was buried.

11. Robert Small's business ventures included a store to help freedmen, the Enterprise Railway, the purchasing of a building for a school for African-American children, and the Beaufort Southern Standard, a black-owned newspaper.

12. Robert Smalls has been honored and recognized by having schools name after him, having a fort named after him, having a ship named after him, having a highway named after him and in many other ways.

*The source of this information is Wikipedia.

LEAVING CHARLESTON HARBOR QUIZ

1. In what state was Robert Smalls Born?
   Ⓐ North Carolina
   Ⓑ Virginia
   Ⓒ South Carolina
   Ⓓ Hawaii

2. What was the name of the ship Robert Smalls steered to freedom?
   Ⓐ The Titanic
   Ⓑ The Yankee Clipper
   Ⓒ The Planter
   Ⓓ The Onward

3. Whose clothing did Robert Smalls did put on?
   Ⓐ The Lieutenant's
   Ⓑ The Master's
   Ⓒ The President's
   Ⓓ The Captain's

4. What Blockade did Robert Smalls have to reach to be free?

Ⓐ Confederate

Ⓑ Union

Ⓒ West Virginia

Ⓓ Turnpike

5. Which direction did Robert Smalls travel on the ship?
Ⓐ North
Ⓑ South
Ⓒ East
Ⓓ West

6. What government office did Robert Smalls attain?
Ⓐ President
Ⓑ Vice-President
Ⓒ Governor
Ⓓ Congressman

7. Which part of the Country's oppression did Robert Smalls escape?
Ⓐ North
Ⓑ South
Ⓒ East
Ⓓ West

8. To say Robert Smalls was genius means that he was what?
Ⓐ Handsome
Ⓑ Athletic
Ⓒ Smart
Ⓓ Tall

9. Which of these professions did Robert Smalls hold?
Ⓐ Doctor
Ⓑ Lawyer
Ⓒ Accountant
Ⓓ Business Owner

10. The book, Leaving Charleston Harbor, shows a statute of whom?
Ⓐ Abraham Lincoln
Ⓑ George Washington
Ⓒ Barak Obama
Ⓓ Robert Smalls

WORDS TO LIVE BY

Train up a child in the way he should go: and when he is old, he will not depart from it (Proverbs 22:6, King James Version).

I can do all things through Christ which strengtheneth me (Philippians 4:13, King James Version).

www.ingramcontent.com/pod-product-compliance
Lightning Source LLC
Chambersburg PA
CBHW041438010526
44118CB00002B/110